ANIMALS ARE AMAZING

MONKEYS

BY VALERIE BODDEN

W

FRANKLIN WATTS
LONDON•SYDNEY

First published in the UK in 2012 by
Franklin Watts
338 Euston Road
London NW1 3BH

Franklin Watts Australia
Level 17/207 Kent Street
Sydney NSW 2000

First published by Creative Education,
an imprint of the Creative Company.

ISBN 978 1 4451 1085 1
Dewey number: 599.8

A CIP catalogue record for this book
is available from the British Library.

Printed in China

Franklin Watts is a division of
Hachette Children's Books
an Hachette UK company
www.hachette.co.uk

Photographs by Alamy (Mike Hill), Corbis (Gallo
Images, Gopal Chitrakar/Reuters, Kevin Schafer),
Getty Images (Rogerio Assis, Ira Block, Tim
Graham, Thorsten Milse, Michael K. Nichols/
National Geographic, Joel Sartore/National
Geographic, Art Wolfe), iStockphoto (Eric Isselée)

CONTENTS

What are monkeys?   4
Different monkeys   7
Big and small monkeys   8
Where monkeys live   11
Monkey food   12
New monkeys   15
Friendly monkeys   16
Noisy monkeys   19
Monkeys and people   20
A monkey story   22
Useful information   24

What are monkeys?

Monkeys are mammals with long arms and legs. Monkeys are very clever and they are good at climbing. There are more than 250 types of monkey in the world.

Monkeys come in lots of different shapes and sizes. This mandrill is the largest type of monkey in the world.

mammals animals that drink milk from their mother as babies.

Different monkeys

Monkeys have long tails. Some monkeys use their tails to help them climb and hang from trees. Monkeys are covered in fur. They come in many different colours. Some are brown or black, others are white or grey. Some are even golden! Monkeys have strong hands and feet. They can bend their fingers and toes to help them climb.

Some monkeys, such as this spider monkey, can use their tail like an extra hand.

Big and small monkeys

Monkeys come in many
sizes. The smallest monkeys are only as
long as a ruler. They weigh less than a
tin of soup. The biggest monkeys can
weigh more than 45 kilogrammes!

*This tiny monkey is very
good at seing in the dark.*

Where monkeys live

These Old World monkeys live in trees in Africa.

Many monkeys live in the **continents** of Africa and Asia. They are called Old World monkeys. Other monkeys live in Central or South America. They are called New World monkeys. Monkeys usually live in trees. **Rainforests** are home to many kinds of monkeys. Other monkeys live in **swamps**. Monkeys can move very quickly from tree to tree.

continents Earth's seven big pieces of land.
rainforests dense forests with many trees and lots of rain.
swamps areas of land where the ground is wet and there are lots of trees.

Monkey food

Monkeys eat plants and animals. Some monkeys like to eat fruit and nuts. Others like to eat insects or birds. Some monkeys even like to eat flowers.

Monkeys are very clever. Some can use sticks or stones to help them find food or break open nuts.

This monkey is eating the flowers on this tree.

New monkeys

Most mother monkeys have one baby at a time. The babies are born with their eyes open. They are able to **cling** to their mother as soon as they are born. Sometimes older monkeys help "babysit" young monkeys. Together, they learn to climb trees and eat food. Wild monkeys can live for more than 15 years.

Mother monkeys teach their babies what is good to eat.

cling holding on to something very tightly.

Friendly monkeys

Monkeys spend most of their day climbing in trees, looking for food. Young monkeys play together. They pretend to fight. Grown monkeys **groom** each other's fur – this shows they care for each other. They sometimes eat the insects that get stuck in their fur!

Grooming each other helps monkeys to keep clean.

groom to get rid of dirt and insects.

Noisy monkeys

Monkeys live in groups, called troops. Some of the troops are small. Other troops can have more than 100 monkeys in them. Monkeys can be very loud! They can whistle and chirp. Other monkeys hoot or howl. They do this to tell each other where they are, or to warn if there is any danger nearby.

It is safer for monkeys, such as baboons, to move around in big groups.

Monkeys and people

People around the world love monkeys. Some people go to the zoo to see monkeys. Other people go to Africa, Asia or South America to see them in the wild. It is fun to watch these playful animals climbing in the trees. Sometimes the monkeys have fun playing with people too!

This Old World monkey, called a proboscis monkey, has a very big nose!

A monkey story

Why do monkeys look like people? People on the continent of Africa tell a story about this. They say that one year, a long time ago, there was very little food. The people put all of their food in a safe place. They asked some strong men to guard it. Some of the men stole the food. The people were angry, so they used magic to turn the men into animals that would look almost like people – monkeys!

Useful information

Read More

Saving Wildlife: Rainforest Animals by Sonya Newland
(Franklin Watts, 2010)

Eco Alert: Rainforests by Rebecca Hunter (Franklin Watts, 2012)

Espresso Ideas Box: Rainforests by Deborah Chancellor
(Franklin Watts, 2011)

Websites

http://www.enchantedlearning.com/themes/monkeys.shtml
This site has monkey activities, facts, and colouring pages.

http://kids.nationalgeographic.com/kids/animals/creaturefeature/howler-monkey/
This site has pictures and information on the howler monkey; the
loudest monkey on the planet!

Every effort has been made by the Publishers to ensure that these websites are suitable
for children, that they are of the highest educational value and that they contain no
inappropriate or offensive material. However, because of the nature of the Internet, it
is impossible to guarantee that the contents of these sites will not be altered. We strongly
advise that Internet access is supervised by a responsible adult.

Index

Africa 11, 20, 22

Asia 11, 20

babies 15

climbing 4, 7, 11, 15, 16, 20

colours 7

continents 11

food 12, 15, 16, 22

fur 7, 16

grooming 16

mammals 4

New World 11

Old World 11, 20

rainforests 11

size 4, 8

sounds 19

swamps 11

tails 7

trees 7, 11, 12, 15, 16, 20

troop 19

zoos 20